A Treatise on Rebuke and Grace

A Treatise on Rebuke and Grace

St. Augustine

A Treatise on Rebuke and Grace

© Lighthouse Publishing 2018

Written by: St. Augustine (Nov.13 354 – Aug.28 430)
Translated by Peter Holmes and Robert Ernest Wallis
Revised by: Professor Benjamin B. Warfield, D.D
Updated into Modern U.S English by A.M. Overett (b. 1960)

All rights reserved. Without limiting the rights under copyright reserved above, no part of this publication may be reproduced, stored in a retrieval system, or transmitted, in any form or by any means (electronic, mechanical, photocopying, recording or otherwise), without the prior written permission of the copyright owner of this book.

Published by
Lighthouse Christian Publishing
SAN 257-4330
5531 Dufferin Drive
Savage, Minnesota, 55378
United States of America

www.lighthousechristianpublishing.com

EXTRACT FROM AUGUSTIN'S "RETRACTATIONS," Book II. Chap. 67, ON THE FOLLOWING TREATISE, "DE CORREPTIONE ET GRATIA."

I Wrote again to the same persons another treatise, which I entitled On Rebuke and Grace, because I had been told that someone there had said that no man ought to be rebuked for not doing God's commandments, but that prayer only should be made on his behalf, that he may do them. This book begins on this wise, "I have read your letters, dearly beloved brother Valentine."

St. Augustine

A TREATISE ON REBUKE AND GRACE,

BY AURELIUS AUGUSTIN, BISHOP OF HIPPO;

In One Book,

Addressed to Valentine, and with him to the monks of adrumetum. a.d. 426 or 427

In the beginning the writer sets forth what is the Catholic faith concerning law, concerning free will, and concerning grace. He teaches that the grace of God by Jesus Christ is that by which alone men are delivered from evil, and without which they do absolutely no good; and this not only by the fact that it points out what is to be done, but that it also supplies the means of doing it with love, since God bestows on men the inspiration of a good will and deed. He teaches that the rebuke of evil men who have not received this grace is neither unjust—since they are evil by their own will—nor useless, although it must be confessed that it is only by God's agency that it can avail. That perseverance in good is truly a great gift of God, but that still the rebuke of one who has not persevered must not on that account be neglected; and that if a man who has not received this gift should relapse of his own will into sin, he is not only deserving of rebuke, but if he should continue in evil until his death, he is moreover worthy of eternal damnation. That it is inscrutable why one should receive this gift and another should not receive it. That of those who are predestinated none can perish. And that the perseverance, which all do not receive who are here called children of God, is constantly given to all those who are truly children by God's foreknowledge and predestination. He answers the question which suggests itself concerning Adam—in what way he sinned by not persevering, since he did not receive perseverance. He shows that such assistance was at the first given to him, as that without it he could not continue if he would, not as that with it it must result that he would. But that now through Christ is given us not only such help as that without it we cannot continue even if we will, but moreover such and so great as that by it we will. He proves that the number of the predestinated, to whom a gift of this kind is appropriated, is certain, and can neither be increased nor diminished. And since it is unknown who belongs to that number, and who does not, that medicinal rebuke must be applied to all who sin, lest they should either themselves perish, or be the ruin of others. Finally, he concludes that neither is rebuke prohibited by grace, nor is grace denied by rebuke.

Chapter 1 [I.]—Introductory. I Have read your letter—Valentine, my dearly beloved brother, and you who are associated with him in the service of God—which your Love sent by brother Florus and those who came to us with him; and I gave God thanks that I have known your peace in the Lord and agreement in the truth and ardor in love, by your discourse delivered to us. But that an enemy has striven among you to the subversion of some, has, by the mercy of God and His marvelous goodness in turning his arts to the advantage of His servants, rather availed to this result, that while none of you were cast down for the worse, some were built up for the better. There is therefore no need to reconsider again and again all that I have already transmitted to you, sufficiently argued out in a lengthy treatise; for your replies indicate how you have received this. Nevertheless, do not in any wise suppose that, when once read, it can have become sufficiently well known to you. Therefore, if you desire to have it exceedingly productive, do not count it a grievance by re-perusal to make it thoroughly familiar; so that you may most accurately know what and what kind of questions they are, for the solution and satisfaction of which there arises an authority not human but divine, from which we ought not to depart if we desire to attain to the point whither we are tending.

Chapter 2. —The Catholic Faith Concerning Law, Grace, and Free Will.

Now the Lord Himself not only shows us what evil we should shun, and what good we should do, which is all that the letter of the law is able to effect; but He moreover helps us that we may shun evil and do good, which none can do without the Spirit of grace; and if this be wanting, the law comes in merely to make us guilty and to slay us. It is on this account that the apostle says, "The letter kills, but the Spirit gives life." He, then, who lawfully uses the law learns therein evil and good, and, not trusting in his own strength, flees to grace, by the help of which he may shun evil and do good. But who is there who flees to grace except when "the steps of a man are ordered by the Lord, and He shall determine his way"? And thus, also to desire the help of grace is the beginning of grace; of which, says he, "And I said, Now I have begun; this is the change of the right hand of the Most

High." It is to be confessed, therefore, that we have free choice to do both evil and good; but in doing evil everyone is free from righteousness and a servant of sin, while in doing good no one can be free, unless he has been made free by Him who said, "If the Son shall make you free, then you shall be free indeed." Neither is it thus, that when any one has been made free from the dominion of sin, he no longer needs the help of his Deliverer; but rather thus, that hearing from Him, "Without me ye can do nothing," he himself also says to Him, "Be thou my helper! Forsake me not." I rejoice that I have found in our brother Florus also this faith, which without doubt is the true and prophetical and apostolical and catholic faith; whence those are the rather to be corrected—whom indeed I now think to have been corrected by the favor of God—who did not understand him.

Chapter 3 [II.]—What the Grace of God Through Jesus Christ is.

For the grace of God through Jesus Christ our Lord must be apprehended, —as that by which alone men are delivered from evil, and without which they do absolutely no good thing, whether in thought, or will and affection, or in action; not only in order that they may know, by the manifestation of that grace, what should be done, but moreover in order that, by its enabling, they may do with love what they know. Certainly, the apostle asked for this inspiration of good will and work on behalf of those to whom he said, "Now we pray to God that ye do no evil, not that we should appear approved, but that ye should do that which is good." Who can hear this and not awake and confess that we have it from the Lord God that we turn aside from evil and do good?—since the apostle indeed says not, We admonish, we teach, we exhort, we rebuke; but he says, "We pray to God that ye do no evil, but that ye should do that which is good." And yet he was also in the habit of speaking to them, and doing all those things which I have mentioned, —he admonished, he taught, he exhorted, he rebuked. But he knew that all these things which he was doing in the way of planting and watering openly were of no avail unless He who giveth the increase in secret should give heed to his prayer on their behalf. Because, as the same teacher of the Gentiles says, "Neither is he that plants anything, neither he that waters, but God that gives the increase."

Chapter 4—The Children of God are Led by the Spirit of God.

Let those, therefore, not deceive themselves who ask, "Wherefore is it preached and prescribed to us that we should turn away from evil and do good, if it is not we that do this, but 'God who worketh in us to will and to do it'?" But let them rather understand that if they are the children of God, they are led by the Spirit of God to do that which should be done; and when they have done it, let them give thanks to Him by whom they act. For they are acted upon that they may act, not that they may themselves do nothing; and in addition to this, it is shown them what they ought to do, so that when they have done it as it ought to be done—that is, with the love and the delight of righteousness—they may rejoice in having received "the sweetness which the Lord has given, that their land should yield her increase." But when they do not act, whether by not doing at all or by not doing from love, let them pray that what as yet they have not, they may receive. For what shall they have which they shall not receive? or what have they which they have not received?

Chapter 5 [III.]—Rebuke Must Not Be Neglected.

"Then," say they, "let those who are over us only prescribe to us what we ought to do and pray for us that we may do it; but let them not rebuke and censure us if we should not do it." Certainly let all be done, since the teachers of the churches, the apostles, were in the habit of doing all, —as well prescribing what things should be done, as rebuking if they were not done, and praying that they might be done. The apostle prescribes, saying, "Let all your things be done with love." He rebukes, saying, "Now therefore there is utterly a fault among you, because ye have judgments among yourselves. For why do ye not rather suffer wrong? Why are ye not rather defrauded? Nay, ye do wrong and defraud; and that, your brethren. Know ye not that the unrighteous shall not possess the kingdom of God?" Let us hear him also praying: "And the Lord," says he, "multiply you, and make you to abound in love one towards another and towards all men." He prescribes, that love should be maintained; he rebukes, because love is not maintained; he prays, that love may abound. O man! learn by his precept what you ought to have; learn by his rebuke that it is by your own fault that you have it not; learn by his prayer whence you may receive what you desire to have.

Chapter 6 [IV.]—Objections to the Use of Rebuke.

"How," says he, "is it my fault that I have not what I have not received from Him, when unless it is given by Him, there is no other at all whence such and so great a gift can be had?" Suffer me a little, my brethren, not as against you whose heart is right with God, but as against those who mind earthly things, or as against those human modes of thinking themselves, to contend for the truth, of the heavenly and divine grace. For they who say this are such as in their wicked works are unwilling to be rebuked by those who proclaim this grace. "Prescribe to me what I shall do, and if I should do it, give thanks to God for me who has given me to do it; but if I do it not, I must not be rebuked, but He must be besought to give what He has not given; that is, that very believing love of God and of my neighbor by which His precepts are observed. Pray, then, for me that I may receive this, and may by its means do freely and with good will that which He commands. But I should be justly rebuked if by my own fault I had it not; that is, if I myself could give it to myself, or could receive it, and did not do so, or if He should give it and I should be unwilling to receive it. But since even the will itself is prepared by the Lord, why dust thou rebuke me because thou sees me unwilling to do His precepts, and dust not rather ask Him Himself to work in me the will also?"

Chapter 7 [V.]—The Necessity and Advantage of Rebuke.

To this we answer: Whoever you are that do not the commandments of God that are already known to you, and do not wish to be rebuked, you must be rebuked even for that very reason that you do not wish to be rebuked. For you do not wish that your faults should be pointed out to you; you do not wish that they should be touched, and that such a useful pain should be caused you that you may seek the Physician; you do not desire to be shown to yourself, that, when you see yourself to be deformed, you may wish for the Reformer, and may supplicate Him that you may not continue in that repulsiveness. For it is your fault that you are evil; and it is a greater fault to be unwilling to be rebuked because you are evil, as if faults should either be praised, or regarded with indifference so as neither to be praised nor blamed, or as if, indeed, the dread, or the shame, or the mortification of the rebuked man were of no avail, or were of any other avail in healthfully stimulating, except to cause that He who is good may be besought, and so out of evil men who are rebuked may make good men who may be praised. For what he who will not be rebuked desires to be done for him, when he says, "Pray for me rather,"—he must be rebuked for that very reason that he may himself also do for himself; because that mortification with which he is dissatisfied with himself when he feels the sting of rebuke, stirs him up to a desire for more earnest prayer, that, by God's mercy, he may be aided by the increase of love, and cease to do things which are shameful and mortifying, and do things praiseworthy and gladdening. This is the benefit of rebuke that is wholesomely applied, sometimes with greater, sometimes with less severity, in accordance with the diversity of sins; and it is then wholesome when the supreme Physician looks. For it is of no profit unless when it makes a man repent of his sin. And who gives this but He who looked upon the Apostle Peter when he denied, and made him weep? Whence also the Apostle Paul, after he said that they were to be rebuked with moderation who thought otherwise, immediately added, "Lest perchance God give them repentance, to the acknowledging of the truth, and they recover themselves out of the snares of the devil."

Chapter 8. —Further Replies to Those Who Object to Rebuke.

But wherefore do they, who are unwilling be rebuked, say, "Only prescribe to me, and pray for me that I may do what you prescribe?" Why do they not rather, in accordance with their own evil inclination, reject these things also, and say, "I wish you neither to prescribe to me, nor to pray for me"? For what man is shown to have prayed for Peter, that God should give him the repentance wherewith he bewailed the denial of his Lord? What man instructed Paul in the divine precepts which pertain to the Christian faith? When, therefore, he was heard preaching the gospel, and saying, "For I certify you, brethren, that the gospel which was preached of me is not after man. For I neither received it from man, nor did I learn it, but by the revelation of Jesus Christ,"—would it be replied to him: "Why are you troubling us to receive and to learn from you that which you have not received nor learnt from man? He who gave to you is able also to give to us in like manner as to you." Moreover, if they dare not say this, but suffer the gospel to be preached to them by man, although it cannot be given to man by man, let them concede also that they ought to be rebuked by those who are set over them, by whom Christian grace is preached; although it is not denied that God is able, even when no man rebukes, to correct whom He will, and to lead him on to the wholesome mortification of repentance by the most hidden and mighty power of His medicine. And as we are not to cease from prayer on behalf of those whom we desire to be corrected, —even although without any man's prayer on behalf of Peter, the Lord looked upon him and caused him to bewail his sin, —so we must not neglect rebuke, although God can make those whom He will to be corrected, even when not rebuked. But a man then profits by rebuke when He pities and aids who makes those whom He will to profit even without rebuke. But wherefore these are called to be reformed in one way, those in another way, and others in still another way, after different and innumerable manners, be it far from us to assert that it is the business of the clay to judge, but of the potter.

Chapter 9 [VI]—Why They May Justly Be Rebuked Who Do Not Obey God, Although They Have Not Yet Received the Grace of Obedience.

"The apostle says," say they, "'For who makes thee to differ? And what hast thou that thou hast not received? Now also if thou hast received it, why dost thou glory as if thou has not received it?' Why, then, are we rebuked, censured, reproved, accused? What do we do, we who have not received?" They who say this wish to appear without blame in respect of their not obeying God, because assuredly obedience itself is His gift; and that gift must of necessity be in him in whom dwells love, which without doubt is of God, and the Father gives it to His children. "This," say they, "we have not received. Why, then, are we rebuked, as if we were able to give it to ourselves, and of our own choice would not give it?" And they do not observe that, if they are not yet regenerated, the first reason why, when they are reproached because they are disobedient to God, they ought to be dissatisfied with themselves is, that God made man upright from the beginning of the human creation, and there is no unrighteousness with God. And thus the first depravity, whereby God is not obeyed, is of man, because, falling by his own evil will from the rectitude in which God at first made him, he became depraved. Is, then, that depravity not to be rebuked in a man because it is not peculiar to him who is rebuked, but is common to all? Nay, let that also be rebuked in individuals, which is common to all. For the circumstance that none is altogether free from it is no reason why it should not attach to each man. Those original sins, indeed, are said to be the sins of others, because individuals derived them from their parents; but they are not unreasonably said to be our own also, because in that one, as the apostle says, all have sinned. Let, then, the damnable source be rebuked, that from the mortification of rebuke may spring the will of regeneration, —if, indeed, he who is rebuked is a child of promise, —in order that, by the noise of the rebuke sounding and lashing from without, God may by His hidden inspiration work in him from within to will also. If, however, being already regenerate and justified, he relapses of his own will into an evil life, assuredly he cannot say, "I have not received," because of his own free choice to evil he has lost the grace of God, that he had received. And if, stung with compunction by rebuke, he wholesomely bewails, and returns to similar good works, or even better, certainly here most manifestly appears the advantage of rebuke. But yet for rebuke by the agency of man to avail, whether it be of love or not, depends only upon God.

Chapter 10—All Perseverance is God's Gift.

Is such a one as is unwilling to be rebuked still able to say, "What have I done, —I who have not received?" when it appears plainly that he has received, and by his own fault has lost that which he has received? "I am able," says he, "I am altogether able, —when you reprove me for having of my own will relapsed from a good life into a bad one, —still to say, What have I done, —I who have not received? For I have received faith, which worketh by love, but I have not received perseverance therein to the end. Will any one dare to say that this perseverance is not the gift of God, and that so great a possession as this is ours in such wise that if anyone has it the apostle could not say to him, 'For what hast thou which thou hast not received?' since he has this in such a manner as that he has not received it?" To this, indeed, we are not able to deny, that perseverance in good, progressing even to the end, is also a great gift of God; and that it exists not save it come from Him of whom it is written, "Every best gift and every perfect gift is from above, coming down from the Father of lights." But the rebuke of him who has not persevered must not on that account be neglected, "lest God perchance give unto him repentance, and he recover from the snares of the devil;" since to the usefulness of rebuke the apostle has subjoined this decision, saying, as I have above mentioned, "Rebuking with moderation those that think differently, lest at any time God give them repentance." For if we should say that such a perseverance, so laudable and so blessed, is man's in such wise as that he has it not from God, we first of all make void that which the Lord says to Peter: "I have prayed for thee that thy faith fails not." For what did He ask for him, but perseverance to the end? And assuredly, if a man could have this from man, it should not have been asked from God. Then when the apostle says, "Now we pray to God that ye do no evil," beyond a doubt he prays to God on their behalf for perseverance. For certainly he does not "do no evil" who forsakes good, and, not persevering in good, turns to the evil, from which he ought to turn aside. In that place, moreover, where he says, "I thank my God in every remembrance of you, always in every prayer of mine for you all making quest with joy for your fellowship in the gospel from the first day until now, being confident of this very thing, that He who has begun a good work in you will perform it until the day of Jesus Christ,"—what else does he promise to them from the mercy of God than perseverance in good to the end? And again where he says, "Epaphras salutes you, who is one of you, a servant of Christ Jesus, always striving for you in prayer, that you may stand perfect and fulfilled in all the will of God,"— what is "that you may stand" but "that you may persevere"? Whence it was said of the devil, "He stood not in the truth;" because he was there, but he did not continue. For assuredly those were already standing in the faith. And when we pray that he who stands may stand, we do not pray for anything else than that he may persevere. Jude the apostle, again, when he says, "Now unto Him that is able to keep you without offence, and to establish you before the presence of His glory, immaculate in joy," does he not most manifestly show that perseverance in good unto the end is God's gift? For what but a good perseverance does He give who preserves without offence that He may place before the presence of His glory immaculate in joy? What is it, moreover, that we read in the Acts of the Apostles: "And when the Gentiles heard, they rejoiced and received the word of the Lord; and as many as were ordained to eternal life believed"? Who could be ordained to eternal life save by the gift of perseverance? And when we read, "He that shall persevere unto the end shall be saved;" with what salvation but eternal? And when, in the Lord's Prayer, we say to God the Father, "Hallowed be Thy name," what do we ask but that His name may be hallowed in us? And as this is already accomplished by means of the laver of regeneration, why is it daily asked by believers, except that we may persevere in that which is already done in us? For the blessed Cyprian also understands this in this manner, since, in his exposition of the same prayer, he says: "We say, 'Hallowed be Thy name,' not that we wish for God that He may be hallowed by our prayers, but that we ask of God that His name may be hallowed in us. But by whom is God hallowed; since He Himself hallows? Well, because He said, 'Be ye holy, since I also am holy;' we ask and entreat that we who have been hallowed in baptism may persevere in that which we have begun to be." Behold the most glorious martyr is of this opinion, that what in these words Christ's faithful people are daily asking is, that they may persevere in that which they have begun to be. And no one need doubt, but that whosoever prays from the Lord that he may persevere in good, confesses thereby that such perseverance is His gift.

Chapter 11 [VII.]—They Who Have Not Received the Gift of Perseverance and Have Relapsed into Mortal Sin and Have Died Therein, Must Righteously Be Condemned.

If, then, these things be so, we still rebuke those, and reasonably rebuke them, who, although they were living well, have not persevered therein; because they have of their own will been changed from a good to an evil life, and on that account are worthy of rebuke; and if rebuke should be of no avail to them, and they should persevere in their ruined life until death, they are also worthy of divine condemnation forever. Neither shall they excuse themselves, saying, —as now they say, "Wherefore are we rebuked?"—so then, "Wherefore are we condemned, since indeed, that we might return from good to evil, we did not receive that perseverance by which we should abide in good?" They shall by no means deliver themselves by this excuse from righteous condemnation. For if, according to the word of truth, no one is delivered from the condemnation which was incurred through Adam except through the faith of Jesus Christ, and yet from this condemnation they shall not deliver themselves who shall be able to say that they have not heard the gospel of Christ, claiming "faith cometh by hearing," how much less shall they deliver themselves who shall say, "We have not received perseverance!" For the excuse of those who say, "We have not received hearing," seems more equitable than that of those who say, "We have not received perseverance;" since it may be said, O man, in that which thou has heard and kept, in that you might persevere if you would; but in no wise can it be said, That which thou has not heard thou might believe if thou would.

Chapter 12. —They Who Have Not Received Perseverance are Not Distinguished from the Mass of Those that are Lost.

And, consequently, both those who have not heard the gospel, and those who, having heard it and been changed by it for the better, have not received perseverance, and those who, having heard the gospel, have refused to come to Christ, that is, to believe on Him, since He Himself says, "No man cometh unto me, except it were given him of my Father," and those who by their tender age were unable to believe, but might be absolved from original sin by the sole laver of regeneration, and yet have not received this laver, and have perished in death: are not made to differ from that lump which it is plain is condemned, as all go from one into condemnation. Some are made to differ, however, not by their own merits, but by the grace of the Mediator; that is to say, they are justified freely in the blood of the second Adam. Therefore, when we hear, "For who makes thee to differ? and what hast thou that thou hast not received? Now, if thou hast received it, why dost thou glory as if thou has not received it?" we ought to understand that from that mass of perdition which originated through the first Adam, no one can be made to differ except he who has this gift, which whosoever has, has received by the grace of the Savior. And this apostolical testimony is so great, that the blessed Cyprian writing to Quirinus put it in the place of a title, when he says, "That we must boast in nothing, since nothing is our own."

Chapter 13. —Election is of Grace, Not of Merit.

Whosoever, then, are made to differ from that original condemnation by such bounty of divine grace, there is no doubt but that for such it is provided that they should hear the gospel, and when they hear they believe, and in the faith which worketh by love they persevere unto the end; and if, perchance, they deviate from the way, when they are rebuked they are amended and some of them, although they may not be rebuked by men, return into the path which they had left; and some who have received grace in any age whatever are withdrawn from the perils of this life by swiftness of death. For He worketh all these things in them who made them vessels of mercy, who also elected them in His Son before the foundation of the world by the election of grace: "And if by grace, then is it no more of works, otherwise grace is no more grace." For they were not so called as not to be elected, in respect of which it is said, "For many are called but few are elected;" but because they were called according to the purpose, they are of a certainty also elected by the election, as it is said, of grace, not of any precedent merits of theirs, because to them grace is all merit.

Chapter 14. —None of the Elect and Predestinated Can Perish.

Of such says the apostle, "We know that to those that love God He worketh together all things for good, to them who are called according to His purpose; because those whom He before foreknew, He also did predestinate to be conformed to the image of His Son, that He might be the first-born among many brethren. Moreover, whom He did predestinate, them He also called; and whom He called, them He also justified; and whom He justified, them He also glorified." Of these no one perishes, because all are elected. And they are elected because they were called according to the purpose—the purpose, however, not their own, but God's; of which He elsewhere says, "That the purpose of God according to election might stand, not of works, but of Him that calleth, it was said unto her that the elder shall serve the younger." And in another place he says, "Not according to our works, but according to His own purpose and grace." When, therefore, we hear, "Moreover, whom He did predestinate, them He also called," we ought to acknowledge that they were called according to His purpose; since He thence began, saying, "He worketh together all things for good to those who are called according to His purpose," and then added, "Because those whom He before foreknew, He also did predestinate, to be conformed to the image of His Son, that He might be the first-born among many brethren." And to these promises He added, "Moreover, whom He did predestinate, them He also called." He wishes these, therefore, to be understood whom He called according to His purpose, lest any among them should be thought to be called and not elected, because of that sentence of the Lord's: "Many the called but few are elected." For whoever are elected are without doubt also called; but not whosoever are called are therefore elected. Those, then, are elected, as has often been said, who are called according to the purpose, who also are predestinated and foreknown. If any one of these perishes, God is mistaken; but none of them perishes, because God is not mistaken. If any one of these perish, God is overcome by human sin; but none of them perishes, because God is overcome by nothing. Moreover, they are elected to reign with Christ, not as Judas was elected, to a work for which he was fitted. Because he was chosen by Him who well knew how to make use even of wicked men, so that even by his damnable deed that venerable work, for the sake of which He Himself had come, might be accomplished. When, therefore, we hear, "Have not I chosen you twelve, and one of you is a devil?" we ought to understand that the rest were elected by mercy, but he by judgment; those to obtain His kingdom, he to shed His blood!

Chapter 15. —Perseverance is Given to the End.

Rightly follows the word to the kingdom of the elect: "If God be for us, who can be against us? He that spared not His own Son, but delivered Him up for us all, how has He not also with Him given us all things? Who shall lay anything to the charge of God's elect? God who justifies? Who condemns? Christ who died? yea, rather who rose again also, who is at the right hand of God, who also solicited on our behalf?" And of how steadfast a perseverance even to the end they have received the gift, let them follow on to say: "Who shall separate us from the love of Christ? shall tribulation, or distress, or persecution, or famine, or nakedness, or peril, or sword? As it is written, Because for thy sake we are killed all the day long, we are accounted as sheep for the slaughter. But in all these things we are more than conquerors, through

Him that hath loved us. For I am certain, that neither death, nor life, nor angel, nor principality, nor things present, nor things to come, nor power, nor height, nor depth, nor any other creature, shall be able to separate us from the love of God which is in Christ Jesus our Lord."

Chapter 16. —Whosoever Do Not Persevere are Not Distinguished from the Mass of Perdition by Predestination.

Such as these were they who were signified to Timothy, where, when it had been said that Hymenæus and Philetus had subverted the faith of some, it is presently added, "Nevertheless the foundation of God stands sure, having this seal, The Lord has known them that are His." The faith of these, which worketh by love, either actually does not fail at all, or, if there are any whose faith fails, it is restored before their life is ended, and the iniquity which had intervened is done away, and perseverance even to the end is allotted to them. But they who are not to persevere, and who shall so fall away from Christian faith and conduct that the end of this life shall find them in that case, beyond all doubt are not to be reckoned in the number of these, even in that season wherein they are living well and piously. For they are not made to differ from that mass of perdition by the foreknowledge and predestination of God, and therefore are not called according to God's purpose, and thus are not elected; but are called among those of whom it was said, "Many are called," not among those of whom it was said, "But few are elected." And yet who can deny that they are elect, since they believe and are baptized, and live according to God? Manifestly, they are called elect by those who are ignorant of what they shall be, but not by Him who knew that they would not have the perseverance which leads the elect forward into the blessed life, and knows that they so stand, as that He has foreknown that they will fall.

Chapter 17 [VIII.]—Why Perseverance Should Be Given to One and Not Another is Inscrutable.

Here, if I am asked why God should not have given them perseverance to whom He gave that love by which they might live Christianly, I answer that I do not know. For I do not speak arrogantly, but with acknowledgment of my small measure, when I hear the apostle saying, "O man, who art thou that replies against God?" and, "O the depth of the riches of the wisdom and knowledge of God! how unsearchable are His judgments, and His ways untraceable!" So far, therefore, as He condescends to manifest His judgments to us, let us give thanks; but so far as He thinks fit to conceal them, let us not murmur against His counsel, but believe that this also is the most wholesome for us. But whoever you are that are hostile to His grace, and thus ask, what do you yourself say? it is well that you do not deny yourself to be a Christian and boast of being a catholic. If, therefore, you confess that to persevere to the end in good is God's gift, I think that equally with me you are ignorant why one man should receive this gift and another should not receive it; and in this case we are both unable to penetrate the unsearchable judgments of God. Or if you say that it pertains to man's free will—which you defend, not in accordance with God's grace, but in opposition to it—that any one should persevere in good, or should not persevere, and it is not by the gift of God if he persevere, but by the performance of human will, why will you strive against the words of Him who says, "I have prayed for thee, Peter, that thy faith fail not"? Will you dare to say that even when Christ prayed that Peter's faith might not fail, it would still have failed if Peter had willed it to fail; that is, if he had been unwilling that it should continue even to the end? As if Peter could in any measure will otherwise than Christ had asked for him that he might will. For who does not know that Peter's faith would then have perished if that will by which he was faithful should fail, and that it would have continued if that same will should abide? But because "the will is prepared by the Lord," therefore Christ's petition on his behalf could not be a vain petition. When, then, He prayed that his faith should not fail, what was it that he asked for, but that in his faith he should have a most free, strong, invincible, persevering will! Behold to what an extent the freedom of the will is defended in accordance with the grace of God, not in opposition to it; because the human will does not attain grace by freedom, but rather attains freedom by grace, and a delightful constancy, and an insuperable fortitude that it may persevere.

Chapter 18. —Some Instances of God's Amazing Judgments.

It is, indeed, to be wondered at, and greatly to be wondered at, that to some of His own children—whom He has regenerated in Christ—to whom He has given faith, hope, and love, God does not give perseverance also, when to children of another He forgives such wickedness, and, by the bestowal of His grace, makes them His own children. Who would not wonder at this? Who would not be exceedingly astonished at this? But, moreover, it is not less marvelous, and still true, and so manifest that not even the enemies of God's grace can find any means of denying it, that some children of His friends, that is, of regenerated and good believers, departing this life as infants without baptism,—although He certainly might provide the grace of this laver if He willed, since in His power are all things,—He alienates from His kingdom into which He introduces their parents; and some children of His enemies He causes to come into the hands of Christians, and by means of this laver introduces into the kingdom, from which their parents are aliens; although, as well to the former infants there is no evil deserving, as to the latter there is no good, of their own proper will. Certainly, in this case the judgments of God, because they are righteous and deep, may neither be blamed nor penetrated. Among these also is that concerning perseverance, of which we are now discoursing. Of both, therefore, we may exclaim, "O the depth of the riches of the wisdom and knowledge of God! how unsearchable are His judgments!"

Chapter 19. —God's Ways Past Finding Out.

Nor let us wonder that we cannot trace His unsearchable ways. For, to say nothing of innumerable other things which are given by the Lord God to some men, and to others are not given, since with Him is no respect of persons; such things as are not conferred on the merits of will, as bodily swiftness, strength, good health, and beauty of body, marvelous intellects and mental natures capable of many arts, or such as fall to man's lot from without, such as are wealth, nobility, honors, and other things of this kind, which it is in the power of God alone that a man should have; not to dwell even on the baptism of infants (which none of those objectors can say does not pertain, as might be said of those other matters, to the kingdom of God), why it is given to this infant and not given to that, since both of them are equally in God's power, and without that sacrament none can enter into the kingdom of God;—to be silent, then, on these matters, or to leave them on one side, let men consider those very special cases of which we are treating. For we are discoursing of such as have not perseverance in goodness, but die in the decline of their good will from good to evil. Let the objectors answer, if they can, why, when these were living faithfully and piously, God did not then snatch them from the perils of this life, "lest wickedness should change their understanding, and lest deceit should beguile their souls"? Had He not this in His power, or was He ignorant of their future sinfulness? Assuredly, nothing of this kind is said, except most perversely and insanely. Why, then, did He not do this? Let them reply who mock at us when in such matters we exclaim, "How inscrutable are His judgments, and His ways past finding out!" For either God giveth this to whom He will, or certainly that Scripture is wrong which says concerning the immature death of the righteous man, "He was taken away lest wickedness should change his understanding, or lest deceit should beguile his soul." Why, then, does God give this so great benefit to some, and not give it to others, seeing that in Him is no unrighteousness nor acceptance of persons, and that it is in His power how long everyone may remain in this life, which is called a trial upon earth?

As, then, they are constrained to confess that it is God's gift for a man to end this life of his before it can be changed from good to evil, but they do not know why it is given to some and not given to others, so let them confess with us that perseverance in good is God's gift, according to the Scriptures, from which I have already set down many testimonies; and let them condescend with us to be ignorant, without a murmur against God, why it is given to some and not given to others.

Chapter 20 [IX.]—Some are Children of God According to Grace Temporally Received, Some According to God's Eternal Foreknowledge.

Nor let it disturb us that to some of His children God does not give this perseverance. Be this far from being so, however, if these were of those who are predestinated and called according to His purpose, —who are truly the children of the promise. For the former, while they live piously, are called children of God; but because they will live wickedly, and die in that impiety, the foreknowledge of God does not call them God's children. For they are children of God whom as yet we have not, and God has already, of whom the Evangelist John says, "that Jesus should die for that nation, and not for that nation only, but that also He should gather together in one the children of God which were scattered abroad;" and this certainly they were to become by believing, through the preaching of the gospel. And yet before this had happened they had already been enrolled as sons of God with unchangeable steadfastness in the memorial of their Father. And, again, there are some who are called by us children of God on account of grace received even in temporal things, yet are not so called by God; of whom the same John says, "They went out from us, but they were not of us, because if they had been of us they would, no doubt, have continued with us." He does not say, "They went out from us, but because they did not abide with us they are no longer now of us;" but he says, "They went out from us, but they were not of us,"—that is to say, even when they appeared among us, they were not of us. And as if it were said to him, Whence do you prove this? he says, "Because if they had been of us, they would assuredly have continued with us." It is the word of God's children; John is the speaker, who was ordained to a chief place among the children of God. When, therefore, God's children say of those who had not perseverance, "They went out from us, but they were not of us," and add, "Because if they had been of us, they would assuredly have continued with us," what else do they say than that they were not children, even when they were in the profession and name of children? Not because they simulated righteousness, but because they did not continue in it. For he does not say, "For if they had been of us, they would assuredly have maintained a real and not a feigned righteousness with us;" but he says, "If they had been of us, they would assuredly have continued with us." Beyond a doubt, he wished them to continue in goodness. Therefore they were in goodness; but because they did not abide in it,—that is, they did not persevere unto the end,—he says, They were not of us, even when they were with us,—that is, they were not of the number of children, even when they were in the faith of children; because they who are truly children are foreknown and predestinated as conformed to the image of His Son, and are called according to His purpose, so as to be elected.

For the son of promise does not perish, but the son of perdition.

Chapter 21. —Who May Be Understood as Given to Christ.

Those, then, were of the multitude of the called, but they were not of the fewness of the elected. It is not, therefore, to His predestinated children that God has not given perseverance for they would have it if they were in that number of children; and what would they have which they had not received, according to the apostolical and true judgment? And thus such children would be given to Christ the Son just as He Himself says to the Father, "That all that Thou hast given me may not perish, but have eternal life." Those, therefore, are understood to be given to Christ who are ordained to eternal life. These are they who are predestinated and called according to the purpose, of whom not one perishes. And therefore, none of them ends this life when he has changed from good to evil, because he is so ordained, and for that purpose given to Christ, that he may not perish, but may have eternal life. And again, those whom we call His enemies, or the infant children of His enemies, whomever of them He will so regenerate that they may end this life in that faith which worketh by love, are already, and before this is done, in that predestination His children, and are given to Christ His Son, that they may not perish, but have everlasting life.

Chapter 22. —True Children of God are True Disciples of Christ.

Finally, the Savior Himself says, "If ye continue in my word, ye are indeed my disciples." Is Judas, then, to be reckoned among them, since he did not continue in His word? Are they to be reckoned among them of whom the gospel speaks in such wise, where, when the Lord had commanded His flesh to be eaten and His blood to be drunk, the Evangelist says, "These things said He in the synagogue as He taught in Capernaum. Many, therefore, of His disciples, when they had heard this, said, This is a hard saying; who can hear it? But Jesus, knowing in Himself that His disciples were murmuring at it, said to them, Doth this offend you? What and if ye shall see the Son of man ascending where He was before? It is the Spirit that quickened, but the flesh profited nothing. The words that I have spoken unto you are spirit and life. But there are some of you who believe not. For Jesus knew from the beginning who were the believing ones, and who should betray Him; and He said, Therefore said I unto you, that no man cometh unto me except it were given of my Father. From this time many of His disciples went away back from Him, and no longer walked with Him." Are not these even in the words of the gospel called disciples? And yet they were not truly disciples, because they did not continue in His word, according to what He says: "If ye continue in my word, then are ye indeed my disciples." Because, therefore, they possessed not perseverance, as not being truly disciples of Christ, so they were not truly children of God even when they appeared to be so, and were so called. We, then, call men elected, and Christ's disciples, and God's children, because they are to be so called whom, being regenerated, we see to live piously; but they are then truly what they are called if they shall abide in that because of which they are so called. But if they have not perseverance, —that is, if they continue not in that which they have begun to be, —they are not truly called what they are called and are not; for they are not this in the sight of Him to whom it is known what they are going to be, —that is to say, from good men, bad men.

Chapter 23. —Those Who are Called According to the Purpose Alone are Predestinated.

For this reason the apostle, when he had said, "We know that to those who love God He worketh all things together for good,"—knowing that some love God, and do not continue in that good way unto the end, — immediately added, "to them who are the called according to His purpose." For these in their love for God continue even to the end; and they who for a season wander from the way return, that they may continue unto the end what they had begun to be in good. Showing, however, what it is to be called according to His purpose, he presently added what I have already quoted above, "Because whom He did before foreknow, He also predestinated to be conformed to the image of His Son, that He might be the first-born among many brethren. Moreover, whom He did predestinate, them He also called," to wit, according to His purpose; "and whom He called, them He also justified; and whom He justified, them He also glorified." All those things are already done: He foreknew, He predestinated, He called, He justified; because both all are already foreknown and predestinated, and many are already called and justified; but that which he placed at the end, "them He also glorified" (if, indeed, that glory is here to be understood of which the same apostle says, "When Christ your life shall appear, then shall ye also appear with Him in glory"), this is not yet accomplished. Although, also, those two things—that is, He called, and He justified—have not been affected in all of whom they are said, —for still, even until the end of the world, there remain many to be called and justified, —nevertheless, He used verbs of the past tense, even concerning things future, as if God had already arranged from eternity that they should come to pass. For this reason, also, the prophet Isaiah says concerning Him, "Who has made the things that shall be." Whosoever, therefore, in God's most providential ordering, are foreknown, predestinated, called, justified, glorified, —I say not, even although not yet born again, but even although not yet born at all, are already children of God, and absolutely cannot perish. These truly come to Christ, because they come in such wise as He Himself says, "All that the Father giveth me shall come to me, and him that cometh to me I will not cast out;" and a little after He says, "This is the will of the Father who hath sent me, that of all that He hath given me I shall lose nothing." From Him, therefore, is given also perseverance in good even to the end; for it is not given save to those who shall not perish, since they who do not persevere shall perish.

Chapter 24. —Even the Sins of the Elect are Turned by God to Their Advantage.

To such as love Him, God co-worketh with all things for good; so absolutely all things, that even if any of them go astray, and break out of the way, even this itself He makes to avail them for good, so that they return lowlier and more instructed. For they learn that in the right way itself they ought to rejoice with trembling; not with arrogation to themselves of confidence of abiding as if by their own strength; not with saying, in their abundance, "We shall not be moved forever." For which reason it is said to them, "Serve the Lord in fear, and rejoice unto Him with trembling, lest at any time the Lord should be angry, and ye perish from the right way." For He does not say, "And ye come not into the right way;" but He says, "Lest ye perish from the right way." And what does this show, but that those who are already walking in the right way are reminded to serve God in fear; that is, "not to be high-minded, but to fear"? which signifies, that they should not be haughty, but humble. Whence also He says in another place, "not minding high things, but consenting with the lowly;" let them rejoice in God, but with trembling; glorying in none, since nothing is ours, so that he who glories may glory in the Lord, lest they perish from the right way in which they have already begun to walk, while they are ascribing to themselves their very presence in it. These words also the apostle made use of when he says, "Work out your own salvation with fear and trembling." And setting forth why with fear and trembling, he says, "For it is God that worketh in you, both to will and to do for His good pleasure." For he had not this fear and trembling who said in his abundance, "I shall not be moved forever." But because he was a child of the promise, not of perdition, he experienced in God's desertion for a little while what he himself was: "Lord," said he, "in Thy favor Thou gave strength to my honor; Thou turned away Thy face from me, and I became troubled." Behold how much better instructed, and for this reason also more humble, he held on his way, at length seeing and confessing that by His will God had endowed his honor with strength; and this he had attributed to himself and presumed to be from himself, in such abundance as God had afforded it, and not from Him who had given it, and so had said, "I shall not be moved forever!" Therefore he became troubled so that he found himself, and being lowly minded learnt not only of eternal life, but, moreover, of a pious conversation and perseverance in this life, as that in which hope should be maintained. This might moreover be the word of the Apostle Peter, because he also had said in his abundance, "I will lay down my life for Thy sake;" attributing to himself, in his eagerness, what was afterwards to be bestowed on him by his Lord. But the Lord turned away His face from him, and he became troubled, so that in his fear of dying for Him he thrice denied Him. But the Lord again turned His face to him, and washed away his sin with his tears. For what else is, "He turned and looked upon him," but, He restored to him the face which, for a little while, He had turned away from him? Therefore he had become troubled; but because he learned not to be confident concerning himself, even this was of excellent profit to him, by His agency who co-works for good with all things to those who love Him; because he had been called according to the purpose, so that no one could pluck him out of the hand of Christ, to whom he had been given.

Chapter 25. —Therefore Rebuke is to Be Used.

Let no one therefore say that a man must not be rebuked when he deviates from the right way, but that his return and perseverance must only be asked for from the Lord for him. Let no considerate and believing man say this. For if such a one is called according to the purpose, beyond all doubt God is co-working for good to him even in the fact of his being rebuked. But since he who rebukes is ignorant whether he is so called, let him do with love what he knows ought to be done; for he knows that such a one ought to be rebuked. God will show either mercy or judgment; mercy, indeed, if he who is rebuked is "made to differ" by the bestowal of grace from the mass of perdition, and is not found among the vessels of wrath which are completed for destruction, but among the vessels of mercy which God has prepared for glory; but judgment, if among the former he is condemned, and is not predestinated among the latter.

Chapter 26 [X.]—Whether Adam Received the Gift of Perseverance.

Here arises another question, not reasonably to be slighted, but to be approached and solved in the help of the Lord in whose hand are both we and our discourses. For I am asked, in respect of this gift of God which is to persevere in good to the end, what I think of the first man himself, who assuredly was made upright without any fault. And I do not say: If he had not perseverance, how was he without fault, seeing that he was in want of so needful a gift of God? For to this interrogatory the answer is easy, that he had not perseverance, because he did not persevere in that goodness in which he was without sin; for he began to have sin from the point at which he fell; and if he began, certainly he was without sin before he had begun. For it is one thing not to have sin, and it is another not to abide in that goodness in which there is no sin. Because in that very fact, that he is not said never to have been without sin, but he is said not to have continued without sin, beyond all doubt it is demonstrated that he was without sin, seeing that he is blamed for not having continued in that goodness. But it should rather be asked and discussed with greater pains in what way we can answer those who say, "If in that uprightness in which he was made without sin he had perseverance, beyond all doubt he persevered in it; and if he persevered, he certainly did not sin, and did not forsake that his uprightness. But that he did sin, and was a forsaker of goodness, the Truth declares. Therefore he had not perseverance in that goodness; and if he had it not, he certainly received it not. For how should he have both received perseverance, and not have persevered? Further, if he had it not because he did not receive it, what sin did he commit by not persevering, if he did not receive perseverance? For it cannot be said that he did not receive it, because he was not separated by the bestowal of grace from the mass of perdition. Because that mass of perdition did not as yet exist in the human race before he had sinned from whom the corrupted source was derived."

Chapter 27. —The Answer.

Wherefore we most wholesomely confess what we most correctly believe, that the God and Lord of all things, who in His strength created all things good, and foreknew that evil things would arise out of good, and knew that it pertained to His most omnipotent goodness even to do good out of evil things rather than not to allow evil things to be at all, so ordained the life of angels and men that in it He might first of all show what their free will was capable of, and then what the kindness of His grace and the judgment of His righteousness was capable of. Finally, certain angels, of whom the chief is he who is called the devil, became by free will outcasts from the Lord God. Yet although they fled from His goodness, wherein they had been blessed, they could not flee from His judgment, by which they were made most wretched. Others, however, by the same free will stood fast in the truth, and merited the knowledge of that most certain truth that they should never fall. For if from the Holy Scriptures we have been able to attain the knowledge that none of the holy angels shall fall evermore, how much more have they themselves attained this knowledge by the truth more sublimely revealed to them! Because to us is promised a blessed life without end, and equality with the angels, from which promise we are certified that when after judgment we shall have come to that life, we shall not fall from it; but if the angels are ignorant of this truth concerning themselves, we shall not be their equals, but more blessed than they. But the Truth has promised us equality with them. It is certain, then, that they have known this by sight, which we have known by faith, to wit, that there shall be now no more any fall of any holy angel. But the devil and his angels, although they were blessed before they fell, and did not know that they should fall unto misery,—there was still something which might be added to their blessedness, if by free will they had stood in the truth, until they should receive that fulness of the highest blessing as the reward of that continuance; that is, that by the great abundance of the love of God, given by the Holy Spirit, they should absolutely not be able to fall any more, and that they should know this with complete certainty concerning themselves. They had not this plenitude of blessedness; but since they were ignorant of their future misery, they enjoyed a blessedness which was less, indeed, but still without any defect. For if they had known their future fall and eternal punishment, they certainly could not have been blessed; since the fear of so great an evil as this would compel them even then to be miserable.

Chapter 28. —The First Man Himself Also Might Have Stood by His Free Will.

Thus also He made man with free will; and although ignorant of his future fall, yet therefore happy, because he thought it was in his own power both not to die and not to become miserable. And if he had willed by his own free will to continue in this state of uprightness and freedom from sin, assuredly without any experience of death and of unhappiness he would have received by the merit of that continuance the fulness of blessing with which the holy angels also are blessed; that is, the impossibility of falling any more, and the knowledge of this with absolute certainty. For even he himself could not be blessed although in Paradise, nay, he would not be there, where it would not become him to be miserable, if the foreknowledge of his fall had made him wretched with the dread of such a disaster. But because he forsook God of his free will, he experienced the just judgment of

God, that with his whole race, which being as yet all placed in him had sinned with him, he should be condemned. For as mary of this race as are delivered by God's grace are certainly delivered from the condemnation in which they are already held bound. Whence, even if none should be delivered, no one could justly blame the judgment of God. That, therefore, in comparison of those that perish few, but in their absolute number many, are delivered, is affected by grace, is affected freely: thanks must be given, because it is affected, so that no one may be lifted up as of his own deserving, but that every mouth may be stopped, and he that glories may glory in the Lord.

Chapter 29 [XI.]—Distinction Between the Grace Given Before and After the Fall.

What then? Did not Adam have the grace of God? Yes, truly, he had it largely, but of a different kind. He was placed amid benefits which he had received from the goodness of his Creator; for he had not procured those benefits by his own deserving; in which benefits he suffered absolutely no evil. But saints in this life, to whom pertains this grace of deliverance, are in the midst of evils out of which they cry to God, "Deliver us from evil." He in those benefits needed not the death of Christ: these, the blood of that Lamb absolves from guilt, as well inherited as their own. He had no need of that assistance which they implore when they say, "I see another law in my members warring against the law of my mind, and making me captive in the law of sin which is in my members. O wretched man that I am! who shall deliver me from the body of this death? The grace of God through Jesus Christ our Lord." Because in them the flesh lusted against the spirit, and the spirit against the flesh, and as they labor and are imperiled in such a contest, they ask that by the grace of Christ the strength to fight and to conquer may be given them. He, however, tempted and disturbed in no such conflict concerning himself against himself, in that position of blessedness enjoyed his peace with himself.

Chapter 30. —The Incarnation of the Word.

Hence, although these do not now require a grace more joyous for the present, they nevertheless need a more powerful grace; and what grace is more powerful than the only begotten Son of God, equal to the Father and co-eternal, made man for them, and, without any sin of His own, either original or actual, crucified by men who were sinners? And although He rose again on the third day, never to die any more, He yet bore death for men and gave life to the dead, so that redeemed by His blood, having received so great and such a pledge, they could say, "If God be for us, who is against us? He who spared not His own Son, but delivered Him up for us all, how has He not with Him also given to us all things?" God therefore took upon Him our nature—that is, the rational soul and flesh of the man Christ—by an undertaking singularly marvelous, or marvelously singular; so that with no preceding merits of His own righteousness He might in such wise be the Son of God from the beginning, in which He had begun to be man, that He, and the Word which is without beginning, might be one person. For there is no one blinded by such ignorance of this matter and the Faith as to dare to say that, although born of the Holy Spirit and the Virgin Mary the Son of man, yet of His own free will by righteous living and by doing good works, without sin, He deserved to be the Son of God; in opposition to the gospel, which says, "The Word was made flesh." For where was this made flesh except in the Virginal womb, whence was the beginning of the man Christ? And, moreover, when the Virgin asked how that should come to pass which was told her by the angel, the angel answered, "The Holy Ghost shall come over on to thee and the power of the Highest shall overshadow thee, therefore that holy thing that shall be born of thee shall be called the Son of God." "Therefore," he said; not because of works of which certainly of a yet unborn infant there are none; but "therefore," because "the Holy Ghost shall come over on to thee, and the power of the Highest shall overshadow thee, that holy thing which shall be born of thee shall be called the Son of God." That nativity, absolutely gratuitous, conjoined, in the unity of the person, man to God, flesh to the Word! Good works followed that nativity; good works did not merit it. For it was in no wise to be feared that the human nature taken up by God the Word in that ineffable manner into a unity of person, would sin by free choice of will, since that taking up itself was such that the nature of man so taken up by God would admit into itself no movement of an evil will. Through this Mediator God makes known that He makes those whom He redeemed by His blood from evil, everlastingly good; and Him He in such wise assumed that He never would be evil, and, not being made out of evil, would always be good.

Chapter 31. —The First Man Had Received the Grace Necessary for His Perseverance, But Its Exercise Was Left in His Free Choice.

The first man had not that grace by which he should never will to be evil; but assuredly he had that in which if he willed to abide he would never be evil, and without which, moreover, he could not by free will be good, but which, nevertheless, by free will he could forsake. God, therefore, did not will even him to be without His grace, which He left in his free will; because free will is sufficient for evil, but is too little for good, unless it is aided by Omnipotent Good. And if that man had not forsaken that assistance of his free will, he would always have been good; but he forsook it, and he was forsaken. Because such was the nature of the aid, that he could forsake it when he would, and that he could continue in it if he would; but not such that it could be brought about that he would. This first is the grace which was given to the first Adam; but more powerful than this is that in the second Adam. For the first is that whereby it is affected that a man may have righteousness if he will; the second, therefore, can do more than this, since by it it is even affected that he will, and will so much, and love with such ardor, that by the will of the Spirit he overcomes the will of the flesh, that lusted in opposition to it. Nor was that, indeed, a small grace by which was demonstrated even the power of free will, because man was so assisted that without this assistance he could not continue in good, but could forsake this assistance if he would. But this latter grace is by so much the greater, that it is too little for a man by its means to regain his lost freedom; it is too little, finally, not to be able without it either to apprehend the good or to continue in good if he will, unless he is also made to will.

Chapter 32. —The Gifts of Grace Conferred on Adam in Creation.

At that time, therefore, God had given to man a good will, because in that will He had made him, since He had made him upright. He had given help without which he could not continue therein if he would; but that he should will, He left in his free will. He could therefore continue if he would, because the help was not wanting whereby he could, and without which he could not, perseveringly hold fast the good which he would. But that he willed not to continue is absolutely the fault of him whose merit it would have been if he had willed to continue; as the holy angels did, who, while others fell by free will, themselves by the same free will stood, and deserved to receive the due reward of this continuance— to wit, such a fulness of blessing that by it they might have the fullest certainty of always abiding in it. If, however, this help had been wanting, either to angel or to man when they were first made, since their nature was not made such that without the divine help it could abide if it would, they certainly would not have fallen by their own fault, because the help would have been wanting without which they could not continue. At the present time, however, to those to whom such assistance is wanting, it is the penalty of sin; but to those to whom it is given, it is given of grace, not of debt; and by so much the more is given through Jesus Christ our Lord to those to whom it has pleased God to give it, that not only we have that help without which we cannot continue even if we will, but, moreover, we have so great and such a help as to will. Because by this grace of God there is caused in us, in the reception of good and in the persevering hold of it, not only to be able to do what we will, but even to will to do what we are able. But this was not the case in the first man; for the one of these things was in him, but the other was not. For he did not need grace to receive good, because he had not yet lost it; but he needed the aid of grace to continue in it, and without this aid he could not do this at all; and he had received the ability if he would, but he had not the will for what he could; for if he had possessed it, he would have persevered. For he could persevere if he would; but that he would not was the result of free will, which at that time was in such wise free that he was capable of willing well and ill. For what shall be more free than free will, when it shall not be able to serve sin? and this should be to man also as it was made to the holy angels, the reward of deserving. But now that good deserving has been lost by sin, in those who are delivered that has become the gift of grace which would have been the reward of deserving.

Chapter 33 [XII.]—What is the Difference Between the Ability Not to Sin, to Die, and Forsake Good, and the Inability to Sin, to Die, and to Forsake Good?

On which account we must consider with diligence and attention in what respect those pairs differ from one another, —to be able not to sin, and not to be able to sin; to be able not to die, and not to be able to die; to be able not to forsake good, and not to be able to forsake good. For the first man was able not to sin, was able not to die, was able not to forsake good. Are we to say that he who had such a free will could not sin? Or that he to whom it was said, "If thou shalt sin thou shalt die by death," could not die? Or that he could not forsake good, when he would forsake this by sinning, and so die? Therefore, the first liberty of the will was to be able not to sin, the last will be much greater, not to be able to sin; the first immortality was to be able not to die, the last will be much greater, not to be able to die; the first was the power of perseverance, to be able not to forsake good—the last will be the felicity of perseverance, not to be able to forsake good. But because the last blessings will be preferable and better, were those first ones, therefore, either no blessings at all, or trifling ones?

Chapter 34. —The Aid Without Which a Thing Does Not Come to Pass, and the Aid with Which a Thing Comes to Pass.

Moreover, the aids themselves are to be distinguished. The aid without which a thing does not come to pass is one thing, and the aid by which a thing comes to pass is another. For without food we cannot live; and yet although food should be at hand, it would not cause a man to live who should will to die. Therefore, the aid of food is that without which it does not come to pass that we live, not that by which it comes to pass that we live. But, indeed, when the blessedness which a man has not is given him, he becomes at once blessed. For the aid is not only that without which that does not happen, but also with which that does happen for the sake of which it is given. Wherefore this is an assistance both by which it comes to pass, and without which it does not come to pass; because, on the one hand, if blessedness should be given to a man, he becomes at once blessed; and, on the other, if it should never be given he will never be so. But food does not of necessity cause a man to live, and yet without it he cannot live. Therefore to the first man, who, in that good in which he had been made upright, had received the ability not to sin, the ability not to die, the ability not to forsake that good itself, was given the aid of perseverance, —not that by which it should be brought about that he should persevere, but that without which he could not of free will persevere. But now to the saints predestinated to the kingdom of God by God's grace, the aid of perseverance that is given is not such as the former, but such that to them perseverance itself is bestowed; not only so that without that gift they cannot persevere, but, moreover, so that by means of this gift they cannot help persevering. For not only did He say, "Without me ye can do nothing," but He also said, "Ye have not chosen me, but I have chosen you, and ordained you that ye should go and bring forth fruit, and that your fruit should remain." By which words He showed that He had given them not only righteousness, but perseverance therein. For when Christ thus ordained them that they should go and bring forth fruit, and that their fruit should remain, who would dare to say, It shall not remain? Who would dare to say, Perchance it will not remain? "For the gifts and calling of God are without repentance;" but the calling is of those who are called according to the purpose. When Christ intercedes, therefore, on behalf of these, that their faith should not fail, doubtless it will not fail unto the end. And thus it shall persevere even unto the end; nor shall the end of this life find it anything but continuing.

Chapter 35. —There is a Greater Freedom Now in the Saints Than There Was Before in Adam.

Certainly, a greater liberty is necessary in the face of so many and so great temptations, which had no existence in Paradise, —a liberty fortified and confirmed by the gift of perseverance, so that this world, with all its loves, its fears, its errors, may be overcome: the martyrdoms of the saints have taught this. In fine, he [Adam], not only with nobody to make him afraid, but, moreover, despite the authority of God's fear, using free will, did not stand in such a state of happiness, in such a facility of [not] sinning. But these [the saints], I say, not under the fear of the world, but despite the rage of the world lest they should stand, stood firm in the faith; while he could see the good things present which he was going to forsake, they could not see the good things future which they were going to receive. Whence is this, save by the gift of Him from whom they obtained mercy to be faithful; from whom they received the spirit, not of fear, whereby they would yield to the persecutors, but of power, and of love, and of continence, in which they could overcome all threatening, all seductions, all torments? To him, therefore, without any sin, was given the free will with which he was created; and he made it to serve sin. But although the will of these had been the servant of sin, it was delivered by Him who said, "If the Son shall make you free, then shall ye be free indeed." And by that grace they receive so great a freedom, that although as long as they live here they are fighting against sinful lusts, and some sins creep upon them unawares, on account of which they daily say, "Forgive us our debts," yet they do not any more obey the sin which is unto death, of which the Apostle John says, "There is a sin unto death: I do not say that he shall pray for it." Concerning which sin (since it is not expressed) many and different notions may be entertained. I, however, say, that sin is to forsake even unto death the faith which worketh by love. This sin they no longer serve who are not in the first condition, as Adam, free; but are freed by the grace of God through the second Adam, and by that deliverance have that free will which enables them to serve God, not that by which they may be made captive by the devil. From being made free from sin they have become the servants of righteousness, in which they will stand till the end, by the gift to them of perseverance from Him who foreknew them, and predestinated them, and called them according to His purpose, and justified them, and glorified them, since He has even already formed those things that are to come which He promised concerning them. And when He promised, "Abraham believed Him, and it was counted unto him for righteousness." For "he gave glory to God, most fully believing," as it is written, "that what He has promised He is able also to perform."

Chapter 36. —God Not Only Foreknows that Men Will Be Good, But Himself Makes Them So.

It is He Himself, therefore, that makes those men good, to do good works. For He did not promise them to Abraham because He foreknew that of themselves they would be good. For if this were the case, what He promised was not His, but theirs. But it was not thus that Abraham believed, but "he was not weak in faith, giving glory to God;" and "most fully believing that what He has promised He is able also to perform." He does not say,

"What He foreknew, He is able to promise;" nor "What He foretold, He is able to manifest;" nor "What He promised, He is able to foreknow:" but "What He promised, He is able also to do." It is He, therefore, who makes them to persevere in good, who makes them good. But they who fall and perish have never been in the number of the predestinated. Although, then, the apostle might be speaking of all persons regenerated and living piously when he said, "Who art thou that judges another man's servant? To his own master he stands or falls;" yet he at once had regard to the predestinated, and said, "But he shall stand;" and that they might not arrogate this to themselves, he says, "For God is able to make him stand." It is He Himself, therefore, that gives perseverance, who can establish those who stand, so that they may stand fast with the greatest perseverance; or to restore those who have fallen, for "the Lord sets up those who are broken down."

Chapter 37. —To a Sound Will is Committed the Power of Persevering or of Not Persevering.

As, therefore, the first man did not receive this gift of God,—that is, perseverance in good, but it was left in his choice to persevere or not to persevere, his will had such strength,—inasmuch as it had been created without any sin, and there was nothing in the way of concupiscence of himself that withstood it,—that the choice of persevering could worthily be entrusted to such goodness and to such facility in living well. But God at the same time foreknew what he would do in unrighteousness; foreknew, however, but did not compel him to this; but at the same time He knew what He

Himself would do in righteousness concerning him. But now, since that great freedom has been lost by the desert of sin, our weakness has remained to be aided by still greater gifts. For it pleased God, in order most effectually to quench the pride of human presumption, "that no flesh should glory in His presence"—that is, "no man." But whence should flesh not glory in His presence, save concerning its merits? Which, indeed, it might have had, but lost; and lost by that very means whereby it might have had them, that is, by its free will; because of which there remains nothing to those who are to be delivered, save the grace of the Deliverer. Thus, therefore, no flesh glories in His presence. For the unrighteous do not glory, since they have no ground of glory; nor the righteous, because they have a ground from Him, and have no glory of theirs, but Himself, to whom they say, "My glory, and the lifter up of my head." And thus it is that what is written pertains to every man, "that no flesh should glory in His presence." To the righteous, however, pertains that Scripture: "He that glories, let him glory in the Lord." For this the apostle most manifestly showed, when, after saying "that no flesh should glory in His presence," lest the saints should suppose that they had been left without any glory, he presently added, "But of Him are ye in Christ Jesus, who of God is made unto us wisdom, and righteousness, and sanctification, and redemption: that, according as it is written, He that glories, let him glory in the Lord." Hence it is that in this abode of miseries, where trial is the life of man upon the earth, "strength is made perfect in weakness." What strength, save "that he that glories should glory in the Lord"?

Chapter 38. —What is the Nature of the Gift of Perseverance that is Now Given to the Saints.

And thus God willed that His saints should not— even concerning perseverance in goodness itself—glory in their own strength, but in Himself, who not only gives them aid such as He gave to the first man, without which they cannot persevere if they will, but causes in them also the will; that since they will not persevere unless they both can and will, both the capability and the will to persevere should be bestowed on them by the liberality of divine grace. Because by the Holy Spirit their will is so much enkindled that they therefore can, because they so will; and they therefore so will because God works in them to will. For if in so much weakness of this life (in which weakness, however, for the sake of checking pride, strength behooved to be perfected) their own will should be left to themselves, that they might, if they willed, continue in the help of God, without which they could not persevere, and God should not work in them to will, in the midst of so many and so great weaknesses their will itself would give way, and they would not be able to persevere, for the reason that failing from infirmity they would not will, or in the weakness of will they would not so will that they would be able. Therefore, aid is brought to the infirmity of human will, so that it might be unchangeably and invincibly influenced by divine grace; and thus, although weak, it still might not fail, nor be overcome by any adversity. Thus, it happens that man's will, weak and incapable, in good as yet small, may persevere by God's strength; while the will of the first man, strong and healthful, having the power of free choice, did not persevere in a greater good; because although God's help was not wanting, without which it could not persevere if it would, yet it was not such a help as that by which God would work in man to will. Certainly, to the strongest He yielded and permitted to do what He willed; to those that were weak He has reserved that by His own gift they should most invincibly will what is good, and most invincibly refuse to forsake this. Therefore when Christ says, "I have prayed for thee that thy faith fails not," we may understand that it was said to him who is built upon the rock. And thus the man of God, not only because he has obtained mercy to be faithful, but also because faith itself does not fail, if he glories, must glory in the Lord.

Chapter 39 [XIII.]—The Number of the Predestinated is Certain and Defined.

I speak thus of those who are predestinated to the kingdom of God, whose number is so certain that one can neither be added to them nor taken from them; not of those who, when He had announced and spoken, were multiplied beyond number. For they may be said to be called but not chosen, because they are not called according to the purpose. But that the number of the elect is certain, and neither to be increased nor diminished,—although it is signified by John the Baptist when he says, "Bring forth, therefore, fruits meet for repentance: and think not to say within yourselves, We have Abraham to our father: for God is able of these stones to raise up children to Abraham," to show that they were in such wise to be cut off if they did not produce fruit, that the number which was promised to Abraham would not be wanting,—is yet more plainly declared in the Apocalypse: "Hold fast that which thou hast, lest another take thy crown." For if another would not receive unless one should have lost, the number is fixed.

Chapter 40. —No One is Certain and Secure of His Own Predestination and Salvation.

But, moreover, that such things as these are so spoken to saints who will persevere, as if it were reckoned uncertain whether they will persevere, is a reason that they ought not otherwise to hear these things, since it is well for them "not to be high-minded, but to fear." For who of the multitude of believers can presume, so long as he is living in this mortal state, that he is in the number of the predestinated? Because it is necessary that in this condition that should be kept hidden; since here we must beware so much of pride, that even so great an apostle was buffeted by a messenger of Satan, lest he should be lifted up. Hence it was said to the apostles, "If ye abide in me;" and this He said who knew for a certainty that they would abide; and through the prophet, "If ye shall be willing, and will hear me," although He knew in whom He would work to will also. And many similar things are said. For on account of the usefulness of this secrecy, lest, perchance, any one should be lifted up, but that all, even although they are running well, should fear, in that it is not known who may attain,—on account of the usefulness of this secrecy, it must be believed that some of the children of perdition, who have not received the gift of perseverance to the end, begin to live in the faith which worketh by love, and live for some time faithfully and righteously, and afterwards fall away, and are not taken away from this life before this happens to them. If this had happened to none of these, men would have that very wholesome fear, by which the sin of presumption is kept down, only so long as until they should attain to the grace of Christ by which to live piously, and afterwards would for time to come be secure that they would never fall away from Him. And such presumption in this condition of trials is not fitting, where there is so great weakness, that security may engender pride. Finally, this also shall be the case; but it shall be at that time, in men also as it already is in the angels, when there cannot be any pride. Therefore the number of the saints, by God's grace predestinated to God's kingdom, with the gift of perseverance to the end bestowed on them, shall be guided thither in its completeness, and there shall be at length without end preserved in its fullest completeness, most blessed, the mercy of their Savior still cleaving to them, whether in their conversion, in their conflict, or in their crown!

Chapter 41. —Even in Judgment God's Mercy Will Be Necessary to Us.

For the Holy Scripture testifies that God's mercy is then also necessary for them, when the Saint says to his soul concerning the Lord its God, "Who crowned thee in mercy and compassion." The Apostle James also says: "He shall have judgment without mercy who hath showed no mercy;" where he sets forth that even in that judgment in which the righteous are crowned and the unrighteous are condemned, some will be judged with mercy, others without mercy. On which account also the mother of the Maccabees says to her son, "That in that mercy I may receive thee with thy brethren." "For when a righteous king," as it is written, "shall sit on the throne, no evil thing shall oppose itself to him. Who will boast that he has a pure heart? or who will boast that he is pure from sin?" And thus God's mercy is even then necessary, by which he is made "blessed to whom the Lord has not imputed sin." But at that time even mercy itself shall be allotted in righteous judgment in accordance with the merits of good works. For when it is said, "Judgment without mercy to him that hath showed no mercy," it is plainly shown that in those in whom are found the good works of mercy, judgment shall be executed with mercy; and thus even that mercy itself shall be returned to the merits of good works. It is not so now; when not only no good works, but many bad works precede, His mercy anticipates a man so that he is delivered from evils,—as well from evils which he has done, as from those which he would have done if he were not controlled by the grace of God; and from those, too, which he would have suffered forever if he were not plucked from the power of darkness, and transferred into the kingdom of the Son of God's love. Nevertheless, since even that life eternal itself, which, it is certain, is given as due to good works, is called by so great an apostle the grace of God, although grace is not rendered to works, but is given freely, it must be confessed without any doubt, that eternal life is called grace because it is rendered to those merits which grace has conferred upon man. Because that saying is rightly understood which in the gospel is read, "grace for grace,"—that is, for those merits which grace has conferred.

Chapter 42. —The Reprobate are to Be Punished for Merits of a Different Kind.

But those who do not belong to this number of the predestinated, whom—whether that they have not yet any free choice of their will, or with a choice of will truly free, because freed by grace itself—the grace of God brings to His kingdom, —those, then, who do not belong to that most certain and blessed number, are most righteously judged according to their deserving. For either they lie under the sin which they have inherited by original generation, and depart hence with that inherited debt which is not put away by regeneration, or by their free will have added other sins besides; their will, I say, free, but not freed,—free from righteousness, but enslaved to sin, by which they are tossed about by divers mischievous lusts, some more evil, some less, but all evil; and they must be adjudged to diverse punishments, according to that very diversity. Or they receive the grace of God, but they are only for a season, and do not persevere; they forsake and are forsaken. For by their free will, as they have not received the gift of perseverance, they are sent away by the righteous and hidden judgment of God.

Chapter 43 [XIV.]—Rebuke and Grace Do Not Set Aside One Another.

Let men then suffer themselves to be rebuked when they sin, and not conclude against grace from the rebuke itself, nor from grace against rebuke; because both the righteous penalty of sin is due, and righteous rebuke belongs to it, if it is medicinally applied, even although the salvation of the ailing man is uncertain; so that if he who is rebuked belongs to the number of the predestinated, rebuke may be to him a wholesome medicine; and if he does not belong to that number, rebuke may be to him a penal infliction. Under that very uncertainty, therefore, it must of love be applied, although its result is unknown; and prayer must be made on his behalf to whom it is applied, that he may be healed. But when men either come or return into the way of righteousness by means of rebuke, who is it that worketh salvation in their hearts but that God who giveth the increase, whoever plants and waters, and whoever labors on the fields or shrubs, —that God whom no man's will resists when He wills to give salvation? For so to will or not to will is in the power of Him who wills or wills not, as not to hinder the divine will nor overcome the divine power. For even concerning those who do what He wills not, He Himself does what He will.

Chapter 44. —In What Way God Wills All Men to Be Saved.

And what is written, that "He wills all men to be saved," while yet all men are not saved, may be understood in many ways, some of which I have mentioned in other writings of mine; but here I will say one thing: "He wills all men to be saved," is so said that all the predestinated may be understood by it, because every kind of men is among them. Just as it was said to the Pharisees, "Ye tithe every herb;" where the expression is only to be understood of every herb that they had, for they did not tithe every herb which was found throughout the whole earth. According to the same manner of speaking, it was said, "Even as I also please all men in all things." For did he who said this please also the multitude of his persecutors? But he pleased every kind of men that assembled in the Church of Christ, whether they were already established therein, or were to be introduced into it.

Chapter 45. —Scriptural Instances Wherein It is Proved that God Has Men's Wills More in His Power Than They Themselves Have.

It is not, then, to be doubted that men's wills cannot, so as to prevent His doing what he wills, withstand the will of God, "who hath done all things whatsoever He pleased in heaven and in earth," and who also "has done those things that are to come;" since He does even concerning the wills themselves of men what He will, when He will. Unless, perchance (to mention some things among many), when God willed to give the kingdom to Saul, it was so in the power of the Israelites, as it certainly was placed in their will, either to subject themselves or not to the man in question, that they could even prevail to withstand God. God, however, did not do this, save by the will of the men themselves, because he beyond doubt had the most omnipotent power of inclining men's hearts whither it pleased Him. For thus it is written: "And Samuel sent the people away, and everyone went away unto his own place. And Saul went away to his house in Gibeah: and there went away with Saul mighty men, whose hearts the Lord touched. And pestilent children said, Who shall save us? This man? And they despised him, and brought him no presents." Will any one say that any of those whose hearts the Lord touched to go with Saul would not have gone with him, or that any of those pestilent fellows, whose hearts He did not touch to do this, would have gone? Of David also, whom the Lord ordained to the kingdom in a more prosperous succession, we read thus: "And David continued to increase, and was magnified, and the Lord was with him." This having been premised, it is said a little afterwards, "And the Spirit clothed Amasai, chief of the thirty, and he said, We are thine, O David, and we will be with thee, O son of Jesse: Peace, peace be unto thee, and peace be to thy helpers; because the Lord has helped thee." Could he withstand the will of God, and not rather do the will of Him who wrought in his heart by His Spirit, with which he was clothed, to will, speak, and do thus? Moreover, a little afterwards the same Scripture says, "All these warlike men, setting the battle in array, came with a peaceful heart to Hebron to establish David over all Israel." By their own will, certainly, they appointed David king. Who cannot see this? Who can deny it? For they did not do it under constraint or without goodwill, since they did it with a peaceful heart. And yet He wrought this in them who worketh what He will in the hearts of men. For which reason the Scripture premised, "And David continued to increase, and was magnified, and the Lord Omnipotent was with him." And thus the Lord Omnipotent, who was with him, induced these men to appoint him king. And how did He induce them? Did He constrain thereto by any bodily fetters? He wrought within; He held their hearts; He stirred their hearts, and drew them by their own wills, which He Himself wrought in them. If, then, when God wills to set up kings in the earth, He has the wills of men more in His power than they themselves have, who else causes rebuke to be wholesome and correction to result in the heart of him that is rebuked, that he may be established in the kingdom of heaven?

Chapter 46 [XV.]—Rebuke Must Be Varied According to the Variety of Faults. There is No Punishment in the Church Greater Than Excommunication.

Therefore, let brethren who are subject be rebuked by those who are set over them, with rebukes that spring from love, varied according to the diversity of faults, whether smaller or greater. Because that very penalty that is called condemnation, which episcopal judgment inflicts, than which there is no greater punishment in the Church, may, if God will, result and be of advantage for most wholesome rebuke. For we know not what may happen on the coming day; nor must anyone be despaired of before the end of this life; nor can God be contradicted, that He may not look down and give repentance, and receive the sacrifice of a troubled spirit and a contrite heart, and absolve from the guilt of condemnation, however just, and so Himself not condemn the condemned person. Yet the necessity of the pastoral office requires, in order that the terrible contagion may not creep through the many, that the diseased sheep should be separated from the sound ones; perchance, by that very separation, to be healed by Him to whom nothing is impossible. For as we know not who belongs to the number of the predestinated, we ought in such wise to be influenced by the affection of love as to will all men to be saved. For this is the case when we endeavor to lead every individual to that point where they may meet with those agencies by which we may prevail, to the accomplishment of the result, that being justified by faith they may have peace with God,—which peace, moreover, the apostle announced when he said, "Therefore, we discharge an embassage for Christ, as though God were exhorting by us, we pray you in Christ's stead to be reconciled to God." For what is "to be reconciled" to Him but to have peace with Him? For the sake of which peace, moreover, the Lord Jesus Christ Himself said to His disciples, "Into whatsoever house ye enter first, say, Peace be to this house; and if the son of peace be there, your peace shall rest upon it; but if not, it shall return to you again." When they preach the gospel of this peace of whom it is predicted, "How beautiful are the feet of those that publish peace, that announce good things!" to us, indeed, everyone then begins to be a son of peace who obeys and believes this gospel, and who, being justified by faith, has begun to have peace towards God; but, according to God's predestination, he was already a son of peace. For it was not said, Upon whomsoever your peace shall rest, he shall become a son of peace; but Christ says, "If the son of peace be there, your peace shall rest upon that house." Already, therefore, and before the announcement of that peace to him, the son of peace was there, as he had been known and foreknown, by—not the evangelist, but—God. For we need not fear lest we should lose it, if in our ignorance he to whom we preach is not a son of peace, for it will return to us again—that is, that preaching will profit us, and not him; but if the peace proclaimed shall rest upon him, it will profit both us and him.

Chapter 47. —Another Interpretation of the Apostolic Passage, "Who Will Have All Men to Be Saved."

That, therefore, in our ignorance of who shall be saved, God commands us to will that all to whom we preach this peace may be saved, and Himself works this in us by diffusing that love in our hearts by the Holy Spirit who is given to us,—may also thus be understood, that God wills all men to be saved, because He makes us to will this; just as "He sent the Spirit of His Son, crying, Abba, Father;" that is, making us to cry, Abba, Father. Because, concerning that same Spirit, He says in another place, "We have received the Spirit of adoption, in whom we cry, Abba, Father!" We therefore cry, but He is said to cry who makes us to cry. If, then, Scripture rightly said that the Spirit was crying by whom we are made to cry, it rightly also says that God wills, when by Him we are made to will. And thus, because by rebuke we ought to do nothing save to avoid departure from that peace which is towards God, or to induce return to it of him who had departed, let us do in hope what we do. If he whom we rebuke is a son of peace, our peace shall rest upon him; but if not, it shall return to us again.

Chapter 48. —The Purpose of Rebuke.

Although, therefore, even while the faith of some is subverted, the foundation of God stands sure, since the Lord knows them that are His, still, we ought not on that account to be indolent and negligent in rebuking those who should be rebuked. For not for nothing was it said, "Evil communications corrupt good manners;" and, "The weak brother shall perish in thy knowledge, because of whom Christ died." Let us not, in opposition to these precepts, and to a wholesome fear, pretend to argue, saying, "Well, let evil communications corrupt good manners, and let the weak brother perish. What is that to us? The foundation of God stands sure, and no one perishes but the son of perdition." [XVI.] Be it far from us to babble in this wise, and think that we ought to be secure in this negligence. For it is true that no one perishes except the son of perdition, but God says by the mouth of the prophet Ezekiel: "He shall surely die in his sin, but his blood will I require at the hand of the watchman."

Chapter 49. —Conclusion.

Hence, as far as concerns us, who are not able to distinguish those who are predestinated from those who are not, we ought on this very account to will all men to be saved. Severe rebuke should be medicinally applied to all by us that they perish not themselves, or that they may not be the means of destroying others. It belongs to God, however, to make that rebuke useful to them whom He Himself has foreknown and predestinated to be conformed to the image of His Son. For, if at any time we abstain from rebuking, for fear lest by rebuke a man should perish, why do we not also rebuke, for fear lest a man should rather perish by our withholding it? For we have no greater bowels of love than the blessed apostle who says, "Rebuke those that are unruly; comfort the feeble-minded; support the weak; be patient towards all men. See that none render to any man evil for evil." Where it is to be understood that evil is then rather rendered for evil when one who ought to be rebuked is not rebuked, but by a wicked dissimulation is neglected. He says, moreover, "Them that sin rebuke before all, that others also may fear;" which must be received concerning those sins which are not concealed, lest he be thought to have spoken in opposition to the word of the Lord. For He says, "If thy brother shall sin against thee, rebuke him between thee and him." Notwithstanding, He Himself carries out the severity of rebuke to the extent of saying, "If he will not hear the Church, let him be unto thee as a heathen man and a publican." And who has more loved the weak than He who became weak for us all, and of that very weakness was crucified for us all? And since these things are so, grace neither restrains rebuke, nor does rebuke restrain grace; and on this account righteousness is so to be prescribed that we may ask in faithful prayer, that, by God's grace, what is prescribed may be done; and both of these things are in such wise to be done that righteous rebuke may not be neglected. But let all these things be done with love, since love both does not sin, and does cover the multitude of sins.

www.ingramcontent.com/pod-product-compliance
Lightning Source LLC
Chambersburg PA
CBHW052116070526
44584CB00017B/2510